RIKER LYNCH

FAMOUS ENTERTAINER

KATIE LAJINESS

Big Buddy Books

An Imprint of Abdo Publishing
abdopublishing.com

BIG BUDDY POP BIOGRAPHIES

abdopublishing.com

Published by Abdo Publishing, a division of ABDO, PO Box 398166, Minneapolis, Minnesota 55439.
Copyright © 2016 by Abdo Consulting Group, Inc. International copyrights reserved in all countries.
No part of this book may be reproduced in any form without written permission from the publisher.
Big Buddy Books™ is a trademark and logo of Abdo Publishing.

Printed in the United States of America, North Mankato, Minnesota.
102015
012016

THIS BOOK CONTAINS
RECYCLED MATERIALS

Cover Photo: JB Lacroix/Getty Images.
Interior Photos: © ACE/INFphoto.com/Corbis (p. 25); Associated Press (pp. 11, 17, 23, 27);
    © Bettmann/Corbis (p. 23); Michael Buckner/AMA2014/Getty Images (p. 21); Robb D. Cohen/
    Invision/AP (p. 29); Invision/AP Photo (p. 19); Chelsea Lauren/Getty Images (p. 5); Photos 12/
    Alamy (p. 15); Kevin Winter/Getty Images (p. 13); ZUMA Press, Inc./Alamy (p. 9).

Coordinating Series Editor: Tamara L. Britton
Contributing Editor: Marcia Zappa
Graphic Design: Jenny Christensen

Library of Congress Cataloging-in-Publication Data

Lajiness, Katie.
  Riker Lynch / Katie Lajiness.
      pages cm. -- (Big Buddy pop biographies)
  Includes index.
  ISBN 978-1-68078-054-3
1. Lynch, Riker, 1991---Juvenile literature. 2. Rock musicians--United States--Biography--Juvenile
literature. 3. Actors--United States--Biography--Juvenile literature. I. Title.
  ML3930.L894L35 2016
  782.421649092--dc23
  [B]
                        2015030704

CONTENTS

RISING STAR

Riker Lynch is an accomplished singer, actor, and dancer. He sings and plays **bass** in the band R5. Fans around the world love his great singing and cool dance moves!

SNAPSHOT

NAME:
Riker Anthony Lynch

BIRTHDAY:
November 8, 1991

BIRTHPLACE:
Littleton, Colorado

POPULAR ALBUM:
Sometime Last Night

MAJOR APPEARANCES:
Glee, Dancing with the Stars

FAMILY TIES

Riker Anthony Lynch was born in Littleton, Colorado, on November 8, 1991. His parents are Mark and Stormie Lynch.

Riker is the oldest of five children. His brothers are Rocky, Ross, and Ryland. Riker has a sister named Rydel.

DID YOU KNOW
Riker did not always attend public school. Instead, he learned from his mom and dad at home.

WHERE IN THE WORLD?

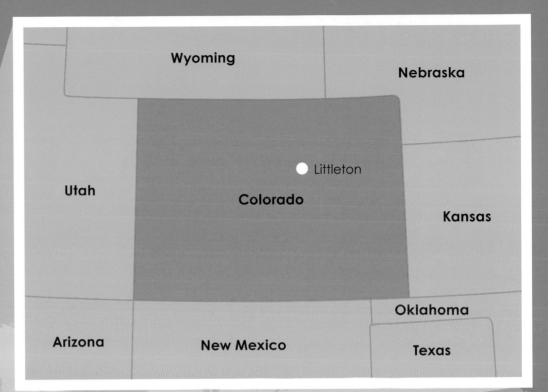

Wyoming

Nebraska

Utah

● Littleton

Colorado

Kansas

Arizona

Oklahoma

New Mexico

Texas

GROWING UP

Even at a young age, Riker was an **entertainer**! He and his **siblings** put on shows for their family. When Riker grew older, he wanted to use his skills on stage. He acted in plays such as *Peter Pan* and *Aladdin*.

Riker's natural talent for singing and dancing led him to play instruments. His siblings also played instruments. Soon, they started to play together.

Riker and his siblings enjoy spending time together as part of the band R5 (*below*).

STARTING OUT

As Riker grew older, he dreamed of being a star. In 2007, he and his family moved to Los Angeles, California.

Riker and his **siblings** took lessons at The Rage **Entertainment** Complex. Famous entertainers such as Taylor Lautner and Ashley Benson also went to this **performing** arts school.

DID YOU KNOW ?
In 2008, Riker got a small part in the DVD movie *Sunday School Musical*.

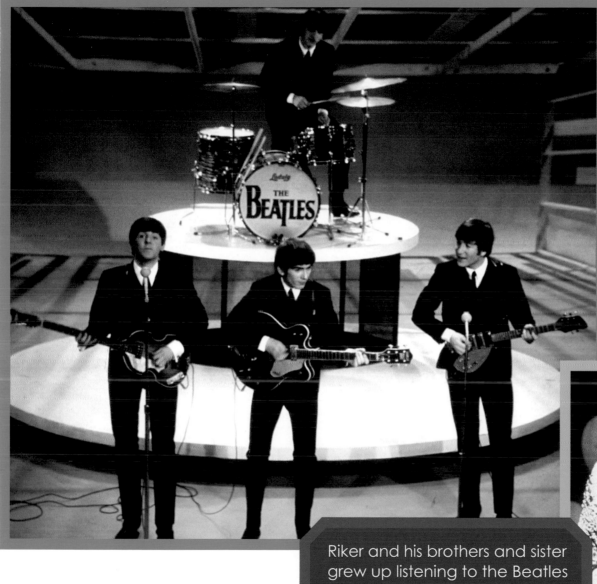

Riker and his brothers and sister grew up listening to the Beatles (*above*) and Elvis (*right*).

Riker's opportunities continued to grow. In 2009, he **performed** with the Rage Boyz Crew on the television show *So You Think You Can Dance*.

In 2011 and 2012, Riker was on the television show *Passport to **Explore***. The show teaches viewers about a city's history and society. On the show, Riker explored cities in northwestern United States and southwestern Canada.

DID YOU KNOW ?
In 2010, Riker danced his way to a television part. He played a dancer on the show *Zeke and Luther*.

The Rage Boyz Crew performed at a show to support the Dizzy Feet Foundation. This group helps provide dance education in the United States.

GLEE

Riker is well-known for his **role** on *Glee*. This television show is about a high school glee club. This is a group that sings short **a cappella** songs.

On the show, the characters are from different social groups. But, they bond over a shared love of singing.

Riker (*right*) played Jeff on *Glee*. Jeff is a member of the a cappella group the Dalton Academy Warblers.

Riker used his singing, dancing, and acting skills on *Glee*. He went along when *Glee* took the show on the road. Riker appeared in the 2011 *Glee Live! In Concert!* tour. He was also in *Glee: The 3D Concert Movie*.

Glee had many fans. Being on the show helped Riker become better known.

R5

Riker and his **siblings** always knew they wanted to **perform** together. So, they formed R5 in 2009. The next year, they self-**released** their first **EP**, *Ready Set Rock*. Fans loved their music! Then, Hollywood Records worked with the band to release their other albums.

Riker (*right*) and R5 have fun on stage. They jump around and dance to the music.

Every member of R5 sings and plays an instrument. Riker plays the **bass**. Rocky and Ross play **guitar**. Rydel plays the keyboard. Their friend Ellington Ratliff is the drummer.

Riker has helped write many R5 songs. The band's songs have fun **lyrics**. R5's popular songs include "Loud," "Heart Made Up On You," and "Smile." R5 **released** albums in 2013 and 2015. The band's latest album is *Sometime Last Night*.

R5 sang their song "Smile" before the 2014 American Music Awards.

FAMILY BANDS

Like R5, many well-known music groups are made up of family members. Over the years, famous family bands have included the Jackson 5, the Osmonds, and Hanson. Today, family bands such as the Band Perry and Kings of Leon have many fans.

Michael Jackson (*front*) and his brothers were the Jackson 5. Michael was the band's lead singer, and grew up to be one of the world's most famous singers!

Hanson is an American band made up of three brothers. In 1997, they had a hit song "MMMBop."

23

DANCING WITH THE STARS

In 2015, Riker's growing fame earned him a spot on the television show *Dancing with the Stars*. On the show, a famous person is paired with a **professional** dancer. Couples **compete** to win a special **trophy**. The public can vote for their favorite couple.

DID YOU KNOW?

Talent runs in Riker's family. Julianne and Derek Hough from *Dancing with the Stars* are Riker's cousins!

Riker appeared on the twentieth season of *Dancing with the Stars*. He was paired with professional dancer Allison Holker (*left*).

Before the **competition** began, Riker and Allison practiced together for many hours. Riker was nervous before their first dance on television. The judges scored Riker and Allison's first dance with 7s and 8s. These were great scores!

Riker and Allison **performed** dances such as the salsa and the foxtrot. Every week, judges and fans voted to keep them on the show. Riker and Allison won second place!

DID YOU KNOW?

Riker and Allison both danced on television before *Dancing with the Stars*. They both started out on *So You Think You Can Dance*.

As dance partners, Riker and Allison appeared at events such as awards shows together.

BUZZ

Today, Riker continues to sing, dance, and act. In 2015, he and Allison were on the television show *Good Morning America*. They danced like they did on *Dancing with the Stars*.

Riker is also busy with his band. R5 started a world tour in summer 2015. They spent a lot of time traveling between cities. Fans are excited to see what Riker Lynch does next!

In 2015, Riker and R5 released the movie *R5: All Day, All Night*. It shows the band in concert and behind the scenes.

GLOSSARY

a cappella without instrumental accompaniment.

bass (BAYS) a stringed musical instrument played by strumming. It is similar to a guitar, but plays lower notes.

competition (kahm-puh-TIH-shuhn) a contest between two or more persons or groups. To compete is to take part in a competition.

entertainment amusement or pleasure that comes from watching a performer. An entertainer is one who provides entertainment.

EP extended play. A music recording with more than one song, but fewer than a full album.

explore to go into in order to make a discovery or to have an adventure.

guitar (guh-TAHR) a stringed musical instrument played by strumming.

lyrics the words to a song.

perform to do something in front of an audience.

professional (pruh-FEHSH-nuhl) working for money rather than only for pleasure.

release to make available to the public.

role a part an actor plays.

sibling a brother or a sister.

trophy (TROH-fee) an award for success.

WEBSITES

To learn more about Pop Biographies, visit **booklinks.abdopublishing.com**. These links are routinely monitored and updated to provide the most current information available.

INDEX